Sociology
FOR THE TWENTY-FIRST CENTURY

SocNotes

Sociology
FOR THE TWENTY-FIRST CENTURY

FIFTH EDITION

Tim Curry
Robert Jiobu
Kent Schwirian

The Ohio State University

PEARSON
Prentice
Hall

Upper Saddle River, New Jersey 07458

© 2008 by PEARSON EDUCATION, INC.
Upper Saddle River, New Jersey 07458

ISBN 0-13-615852-8

Printed in the United States of America

Contents

Sociology
FOR THE TWENTY-FIRST CENTURY

Chapter 1 – What Is Sociology?

1) Chapter Preview

2) The Sociological Viewpoint

3) The Origins of Sociology and Three Central Figures: Karl Marx, Émile Durkheim, and Max Weber

   a) Karl Marx (1919-1883)

   b) Émile Durkheim (1858-1917)

   c) Max Weber (1864-1920)

   d) Marx, Durkheim, and Weber Compared

4) Perspectives Within Sociology

   a) The Functionalist Perspective

   b) The Conflict Perspective

   c) The Symbolic Interaction Perspective

5) Sociology and Social Concerns

6) Sociology's Four Realms

7) The Sociological Imagination

8) Sociology and the Twenty-First Century

9) Looking Ahead

Sociology: A Definition

- The scientific study of social structure and social interaction and of the factors making for change in social structure and social interaction.

The "Sociological Viewpoint" Includes Four Key Concepts

- Science
  - Sociologists follow the scientific method
- Social Structure
  - We are members of social units, or a structure, that endures over time
- Social Interaction
  - How we relate with others is a topic sociologists attempt to understand
- Social Change
  - Continuity and change are normal features of social life

The Origins of Sociology

- Industrial Revolution
  - Technological innovations leads to rearrangements in peoples' lives
- Social and Political Changes
  - Ordinary people gained a voice in social affairs
- Sociology Emerges
  - New sociologists attempt to make sense of this new way of life

Karl Marx

- Lived 1818-1883
- German philosopher
- Writer and social critic
- Personally involved in social change
- Believed social scientists should help to improve society

- Struggle between owners and workers
- Capitalist owners will oppress ordinary people
- Eventually, people become alienated
- People lose control over their lives

Emile Durkheim

- Lived 1858-1917
- Influential French sociologist, educator, and public official
- Studied the ties that bind society together

- Mechanical solidarity
  - Traditional societies are united by social similarities
- Organic solidarity
  - Modern societies are united by interdependence
- Anomie
  - Rapid social change leads to loss of social norms and produces many social problems

Max Weber

- Lived 1864-1920
- German scholar who studied wide variety of topics
- Like other peers, he studied the impact of industrialization on peoples' lives

- Rationalization
  - Traditional societies emphasize emotion and personal ties
  - Modern societies emphasize calculation, efficiency, self control
  - Personal ties decline and people become "disenchanted"

3

Marx, Durkheim, and Weber Compared

- How is life treating you?
  - Marx's alienated person
    - I really don't care (because I'm detached from my work and from other people).
  - Durkheim's anomic person
    - I'm distressed by it (because there are no common rules or norms to guide me).
  - Weber's rational person
    - Let me think about it, and I'll get back to you later (because I need to make some calculations before I know how to answer).

Perspectives within Sociology

- Functionalist
- Conflict
- Symbolic Interaction

The Functionalist Perspective

- Parts of a social system work together to maintain a balance
  - Functions are actions that have positive consequences
  - Dysfunctions are actions that have negative consequences
  - Manifest functions are intended
  - Latent functions are unintended

The Conflict Perspective

- Society is held together by who has power at a moment in time
  - Power allows some to dominate others
  - Dominance leads to conflict
  - Conflict and change are inevitable
  - Conflict holds society together as new alliances are formed and others fail

The Symbolic Interaction Perspective

- Individuals construct the nature of their social world through social interaction
  - Social life is possible only because humans can communicate through symbols
  - All human communications take place through the perception and interpretation of symbols
  - How people define situations is important
  - There is a general consensus on how situations are defined
  - We do not respond directly to reality but to the symbolic meanings we attach to the real world

Sociology's Four Realms

- Basic Science
  - Expanding knowledge
- Critical Sociology
  - Debate, argument, and controversy
- Applied Research
  - Application of knowledge to real-world problems
- Public Activism
  - Working for social change

The Sociological Imagination

- The intellectual ability to discern the relationship between individual experience and social forces in the larger society.
  - Asking questions about:
    - Social structure
    - Human history
    - Demographics

What Is a Concept Web?

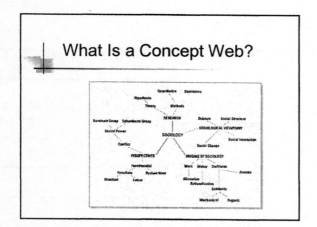

Chapter 2 – Sociological Research Methods

1) Chapter Preview

2) Theory and Hypothesis

   a) Theory

   b) Hypothesis

3) Methodological Requirements and Concepts

   a) Variables and Constants

   b) Nominal and Operational Definitions

   c) Reliability and Validity

4) Research Methods

   a) Quantitative Methods

   b) Controlled Experiment

   c) Qualitative Methods

   d) Participant Observation

   e) Image Analysis

   f) Quantitative and Qualitative Methods Compared

   g) Ethics and Research

   h) Research Methods in the Twenty-First Century

5) Looking Ahead

Theory and Hypothesis

- Theory
  - A body of plausible assertions that scientifically explain a phenomenon
- Hypothesis
  - A prediction that reasonably follows from a theory

Methodological Requirements and Concepts

- Variables and Constants
  - A variable is something that changes or varies
  - A constant does not change
- Nominal and Operational Definitions
  - Nominal: expresses the essence of an idea in words
  - Operational: expresses the essence of an idea in terms of measurement
- Reliability and Validity
  - Reliability: consistency
  - Validity: accuracy

Research Methods: Quantitative Methods

- Survey
  - A population, a group to be studied, is selected
  - A representative sample of that group is surveyed
  - A random sample can be used to obtain generalization
- Controlled Experiment
  - The experimental group is exposed to the intent of the experiment
  - The control group is not exposed to the intent of the experiment

Research Methods:
Qualitative Methods

- Historical Records
  - Does the time in history influence the findings?
  - Are records accurate, complete, and unbiased?
- Interviews and Life Histories
  - Structured interviews seek detailed answers to questions
  - Life histories seek to discover essential features of a lifetime
- Participant Observation
  - Researchers participate in the topic of the study

Ethics and Research

- Scientists must avoid harming people who participate in a study
  - Some questions may produce discomfort or may pry
  - Reprisals may occur if results become known
  - Experiments can grant great power to researchers who may expose subjects to risk

Television in Our Lives

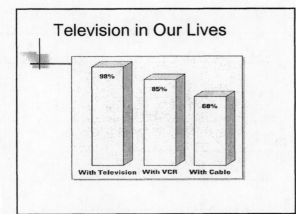

98%   With Television
85%   With VCR
68%   With Cable

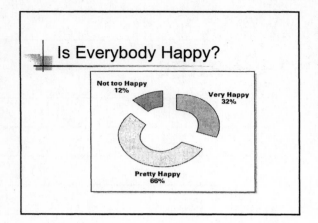

Chapter 3 – Culture, Society, and Social Change

1) Chapter Preview

2) Culture and Society

   a) Values and Norms

   b) Symbols and Language

   c) Ethnocentrism and Cultural Relativity

3) Types of Societies

   a) Hunting and Gathering Societies

   b) Horticultural and Pastoral Societies

   c) Agrarian Societies

   d) Industrial Societies

   e) Postindustrial Societies

   f) Transitional Societies

4) The Great Social Transformation

   a) Communal Relationships

   b) Associational Relationships

5) The Great Social Transformation and This Text

6) Theories of Change and Development

   a) Social Change and the Credit Card

   b) Social Evolution

   c) Functionalism and Social Evolution

   d) Modernization Theory

   e) Conflict Theory and Change: World Systems

7) Catalysts for Change

   a) Human Agency: Individual and Collective

   b) Revolution and War

The Concept of Culture

- Material Culture
  - Physical objects used by people to obtain goals
    - Tools such as computers
    - Buildings
- Nonmaterial Culture
  - Ideas, concepts, art, language, and other symbols
    - Legal codes
    - music

Values and Norms

- Values
  - Preferences about what is good or bad, right or wrong, desirable or undesirable
    - Some examples in the United States include the importance of hard work, individuality, and romantic love
- Norms
  - The specific explanations about how people behave in a given situation
    - Folkways are rules about ordinary matters
    - Mores are rules about serious matters
    - Taboos are rules about extremely serious and unusual situations

Ethnocentrism and Cultural Relativity

- Ethnocentrism: the belief that one's own culture is superior
  - For example, we may conclude that another group is inferior because they prefer certain foods that we consider to be inedible
- Cultural relativism: the belief that each culture is unique
  - Each culture must be judged according to its own terms
  - Multiculturalism, a recent concept, is the belief that cultures should be viewed from different perspectives

Types of Societies: How People Meet Their Basic Needs

- Hunting and Gathering societies
  - Small nomadic groups search for basic needs
- Horticultural and Pastoral societies
  - People who live in small villages and cultivate gardens, or maintain a herd of domesticated animals
- Agrarian societies
  - Plow-based intensive farming producing a food surplus that can support a very large population

Types Continued:

- Industrial societies
  - Technology and mechanization drive mass production
- Postindustrial societies
  - Creation and transmission of highly specialized knowledge related to providing services
- Transitional Societies
  - Societies that are partly agrarian and partly industrial and whose population members are largely peasants

The Great Social Transformation

The Great Social Transformation

- Communal relationships
  - Personal and intimate connections
  - Most social life takes place in family, kin groups, and small communities
  - Traditional and slow to change
- Associational relationships
  - Impersonal relationships based upon shared goals
  - Most social life takes place in larger social units, such as the corporation
  - Traditions decline and change accelerates

Table 3.1

CHARACTERISTICS OF COMMUNAL SOCIETIES	CHARACTERISTICS OF ASSOCIATIONAL SOCIETIES
1. Limited division of labor	1. Complex division of labor in all activities
2. Family, clan, tribe, and village base social units	2. Associations, organizations, and corporations basic units
3. Personalized relationships	3. Relationships formalized, transitory, less personal
4. Economy based on commodities in nearby habitat	4. Economy based on manufacturing and related activities
5. Overall level of technology is low	5. Level of technology is high
6. Political institutions nonbureaucratic	6. Political institutions complex and bureaucratic
7. Limited system of social stratification	7. Complex social stratification—large middle class
8. Rich ceremonial life	8. Rationality prized, diminished role of spirituality
9. Limited contact with other societies	9. Society part of a global network of societies
10. Life in communal societies is a. Less complex b. Less diverse c. More traditional d. More personal	10. Life in associational societies is a. More complex b. More diverse c. Less traditional d. More impersonal

Characteristics of Communal and Associational Societies

Theories of Change and Development

- Culture lag
  - The tendency for the material culture to change more rapidly than the nonmaterial culture
- Social evolution
  - As societies evolve, disruptions occur while equilibrium is sought
- Modernization
  - Assumes that all societies will eventually become industrialized
- World systems
  - A small core of wealthy, powerful nations will dominate and exploit the poorer majority

Table 3.2

PERSPECTIVE	VIEW OF CHANGE AND DEVELOPMENT	KEY CONCEPTS AND PROCESSES
Comparison of Theoretical Perspectives on Change and Development		
Evolutionary theory	Sees societal change as progressing from simple to complex forms	Competition Survival of the fittest Unilinear evolution
Functionalism	Sees societal change as a way to increase efficiency of society	Differentiation Equilibrium Multilinear evolution
Modernization	Sees societal change as inevitable because of benefits of industrialization and advanced technology	Modernization Industrialization
World systems	Sees development and change as a contest of power between industrialized and less-developed nations	Core, periphery, and semiperiphery nations Neocolonialism

---

Causes of Change

- Human agency
  - Collective effort to change a condition
- Revolution and War
  - Violent collective effort to bring about change
- Cultural processes
  - Invention: combining the known into something new
  - Discovery: finding something not known before
  - Diffusion: transmitting knowledge to another culture

Causes of Change (Continued)

- Population
  - Shifts in population can trigger social changes
- Catastrophes
  - Natural events, such as earthquakes, can produce major changes
- Technology
  - New technological innovations lead to other changes

Global Map of the European Voyages of Contact

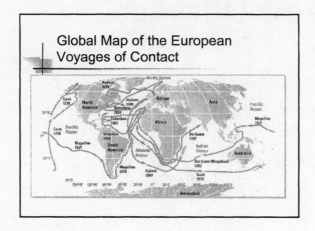

The World's Aging Population

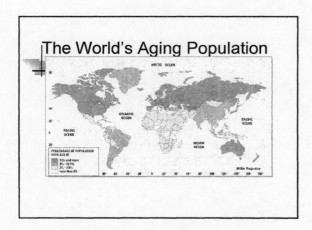

CONCEPT WEB Culture, Society, and Social Change

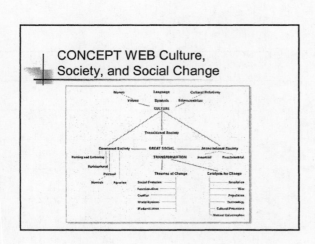

Chapter 4 – Socialization

1) Chapter Preview

2) The Great Social Transformation and Socialization

3) Socialization and the Life Course

    a) Socialization and Stages of the Life Course

    b) Death and Dying

    c) Agents of Socialization

4) Socialization and the Self

    a) Cooley: The Looking Glass Self

    b) Mead: Role Taking

5) Moral Socialization

    a) Sigmund Freud

    b) Erik Erikson

    c) Jean Piaget and Lawrence Kohlberg

    d) Carol Gilligan: Morality and Gender

6) Resocialization and Total Institutions

7) Socialization in the Twenty-First Century

8) Looking Ahead

Socialization

- Learning language, values, rules of our culture
- Develop a sense of self
- Primary socialization includes basic knowledge and occurs in the early years
- Secondary socialization emphasizes advanced knowledge and occurs throughout the life course

Socialization and Stages in the Life Course

- Childhood
  - Elementary formal learning; develop self esteem
- Adolescence
  - Transitional stage from childhood to adult
- Adulthood
  - Life's initial tasks met, peak, moderate
- Old Age
  - Withdraw from long-held roles and resocialize into new ones; disengage or increase participation
- Death and Dying
  - Extending life and confronting death

What Things Do Parents Believe Are Most Important for a Child to Learn to Prepare Him or Her for Life

ITEMS	PERCENT WHO BELIEVE THAT THIS ITEM IS MOST IMPORTANT
To think for himself or herself	53
To obey	18
To work hard	15
To help others when they need help	13
To be well liked or popular	0

SOURCE: The National Opinion Research Center (NORC) (1998).

Agents of Socialization

- Family
  - Most important agent, dominates early process
- School
  - Responsible for formal socialization such as thinking skills
- Peers
  - Informal socialization including testing new roles
- Mass Media
  - Exposure to greater a world either fabricated or real

Cooley and The Looking Glass Self: How Does the Self Emerge?

- How do you think you appear to others?
- How do you think others respond to this image that you have of yourself?
- You respond to the imagined reactions of others
  - If positive, you build
  - If negative, you reject or change

Mead: Taking the Role of the Other Leads to the Development of the Self

- Imitation
  - Young children, lacking a sense of self, imitate others
- Play
  - Around 3 to 6, children pretend, or take on a specific role of someone else
- Game
  - After age 6, children are able to take on multiple roles requiring complex interactions with other roles

20

Comparison of Three Theoretical Perspectives

PERSPECTIVE[a]	VIEW OF SOCIETY AND PROCESSES	KEY CONCEPTS
Functionalism	Sees society as a system of parts that work together to maintain the cohesion of the whole system	Manifest functions Latent functions Dysfunctions Anomie
Conflict Theory	Sees society as a collection of parts held together by social power	Conflict Dominance Inequality Alienation
Symbolic Interaction	Sees society as socially constructed by everyday encounters between people	Symbols Meaning Significant others Definition of the situation

---

Moral Socialization: Freud

- Human behavior contains both conscious and unconscious elements
  - Id: basic drives
  - Superego: our conscience
- The ego manages the id and superego
  - Unresolved childhood conflicts may become disorders
  - Ability to repress inappropriate behavior leads to social acceptance

---

Moral Socialization: Erikson

- Stage 1 (1st year): trust v. mistrust
- Stage 2 (2nd-3rd year): shame v. doubt
- Stage 3 (age 4-5): initiative v. guilt
- Stage 4 (age 6-11): industriousness v. inferiority

- Stage 5 (age 12-20): identity v. confusion
- Stage 6 (age 20-24): intimacy v. isolation
- Stage 7 (age 25-65): generativity v. self absorption
- Stage 8 (65 +): integrity v. despair

Moral Development: Piaget, Kohlberg and Dilemmas

- Piaget: morality develops in two stages
  - Children, under 12, learn to follow adult rules
  - Later, they learn that rules are flexible
- Kohlberg: morality develops in three stages (building upon Piaget)
  - Preconventional: children follow rules to avoid punishment
  - Conventional: most people make social rules personal rules
  - Postconventional: broad principals guide behavior and may conflict with ordinary rules

Morality and Gender: Gilligan

- Men define morality in terms of justice
  - Morality is determined by the logical application of established rules that can be judged right or wrong
- Women define morality in terms of responsibility
  - Morality is determined by an obligation to exercise care, to satisfy needs, and to avoid hurt

Resocialization

- Resocialization often takes place in a total institution
  - A place, such as a prison, where total control over an individual can be created
- Resocialization attempts to destroy an old identity
  - Techniques are used to convince, say, a drug addict that his life is dysfunctional
- Resocialization attempts to build a new identity
  - An entirely new drug-free life is built

CONCEPT WEB Socialization

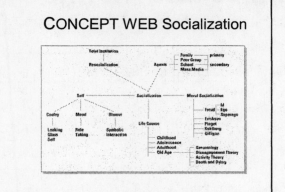

_____

_____

_____

_____

_____

_____

_____

Chapter 5 – Deviance and Crime

1) Chapter Preview

2) The Great Social Transformation and Deviance and Crime

    a) Deviance and Crime

3) Crime Rates

4) Explanations for Deviance and Crime

    a) Functionalist Explanations

    b) Symbolic Interactionist Explanations

    c) Conflict Theory

    d) Demographics

5) The Criminal Justice System

    a) The Police

    b) The Courts

    c) Punishment and Corrections

6) Deviance and Crime in the Twenty-First Century

7) Looking Ahead

The Great Social Transformation and Deviance and Crime

- Deviance and crime are universal
- Deviance is any violation of a widely held norm
- Crime refers to an act that has been declared illegal by some authority
- Communal societies often use restitution
- Associational societies focus on the offender rather than the victim

Deviance and Crime

- Deviance
  - Any violation of a widely held norm
    - Most deviance is mild and typically ignored
    - More serious deviance will attract attention of authorities
- Crime
  - An act that has been declared illegal by some authority
    - Not all deviance is declared to be criminal
    - Criminalizing acts are necessary to prevent upsets of the social order

Social Control

- Internal social controls
  - Parents and other agents of socialization instill in children important social norms
  - Social norms become our own personal moral norms
- External social controls
  - Societal mechanisms are created to prevent deviance including police and surveillance cameras.

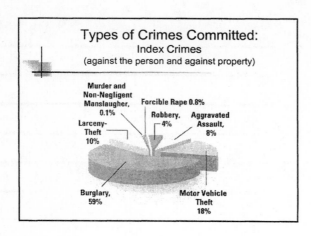

Types of Crimes Committed:
Index Crimes
(against the person and against property)

Murder and Non-Negligent Manslaugher, 0.1%
Forcible Rape 0.8%
Robbery, 4%
Aggravated Assault, 8%
Larceny-Theft 10%
Burglary, 59%
Motor Vehicle Theft 18%

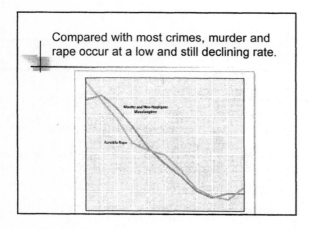

Compared with most crimes, murder and rape occur at a low and still declining rate.

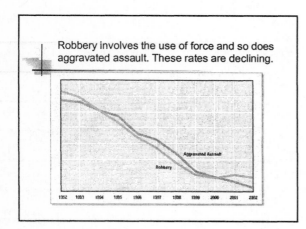

Robbery involves the use of force and so does aggravated assault. These rates are declining.

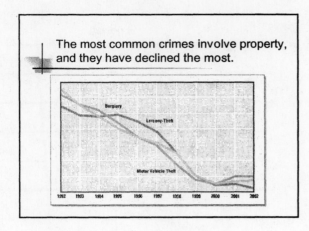

The most common crimes involve property, and they have declined the most.

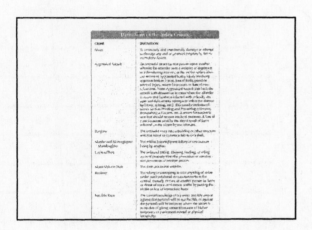

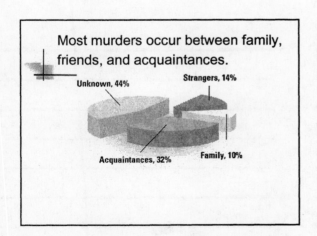

Most murders occur between family, friends, and acquaintances.

Unknown, 44%

Strangers, 14%

Acquaintances, 32%

Family, 10%

How Much Crime?

- Uniform Crime Reports
  - Crimes reported to police
  - Index crimes are those that get special attention and include murder, rape and robbery
- Crimes Not Reported
  - National Crime Victimization Survey
    - People are asked about personal experiences as a crime victim
    - Much crime is not reported

Other Crimes

- Hate Crimes
  - A crime motivated by racial prejudice or other biases
    - May include crimes based upon religion, sexual orientation, ethnicity, disability
    - Thousands are reported each year
- Organized Crime
  - Crime conducted by businesses supplying illegal goods and services
    - Corruption and violence are routinely used
    - May include drug trafficking, illegal immigration, and child prostitution

Hate Crimes

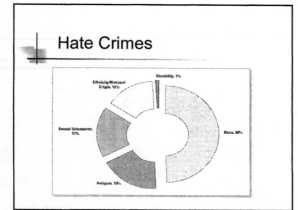

Explaining Crime: Strain Theory

- Strain develops between cultural goals and normal means to obtain them. Reponses include:
  - Conformity: accept both
  - Innovation: accept goals, reject means
  - Ritualism: reject goals, accept means
  - Retreatism: rejects means and goals
  - Rebellion: rejects both, replaces with new

Explaining Crime: Social Bonds

- Why don't people commit crimes?
  - Interpersonal attachments
    - Strong relations with families and organizations result in attachments to existing norms and values
  - Commitment-belief
    - People can become strongly committed to non-deviant activities

Cultural Transmission

- Deviance is learned through socialization
  - Deviance is learned through small, intimate groups
  - Special techniques, motives, drives, and attitudes are learned
  - People develop "mind-sets" that are favorable or not favorable to prevailing norms
  - Frequent, long-term and intense contact with socializing agents increase learning

Labeling Theory

- A definition is attached to an individual
  - The definition is not positive and stigmatizes the individual
  - People begin to respond accordingly to the definition
  - The individual begins to tolerate or accept the label
  - The individual begins to seek the company of like others who reinforce the label

Conflict Theory

- Definitions of crime reflect the interests of the rich and powerful: are laws inherently fair?
  - Vagrancy laws only affect the poor
  - Prisoners are typically poor
  - Gun production and sales make some wealthy yet few protections established for people
  - White collar crime costs the nation far more than street crime

Demographics

- Age
  - Aging-out
    - Half of the people arrested for violent crime and about two-thirds of the people arrested for property crimes are aged 16-25
- Gender
  - Males account for 82 percent of people arrested for violent crimes and 62 percent of people arrested for property crimes

Comparison of Three Theoretical Perspectives on Deviance and Crime		
PERSPECTIVE	VIEW OF DEVIANCE	KEY CONCEPTS AND THEORY
Functionalism	Sees deviance as a threat to the social system; reactions to deviance help define and strengthen the moral foundation of society	Anomie Strain theory
Conflict Theory	Sees laws as reflecting interests of the wealthy and punishments unfairly influenced by race and class	White-collar crime Corporate crime Power and inequality
Symbolic Interaction	Sees deviance as socially constructed by everyday encounters between people	Labeling theory Cultural transmission Differential association Social bonds

Types of Legal Systems

- Common law
  - Legal principles are based on customs
  - Adversarial system; legalized contest
  - Judges follow past rulings
- Civil law
  - Laws imposed by ruler
  - Judges seek to find truth
- Religious law
  - Law is divine will
  - Judges interpret religious principles

The Criminal Justice System

- The Police
- The Courts
- Punishment and Corrections
  - Retribution
    - An act of vengeance to "right the wrong"
  - Deterrence
    - Threat of punishment, or other, to discourage crime
  - Incapacitation
    - Separating a confining criminals
  - Rehabilitation
    - Efforts to reform a criminal

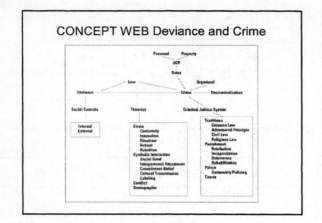

CONCEPT WEB Deviance and Crime

Chapter 6 – Interaction, Groups, and Organizations

1) Chapter Preview

2) The Great Social Transformation and Interaction, Groups, and Organizations

3) Social Interaction

   a) Types of Interaction

   b) Components of Interaction

   c) Role

   d) Sociological Analysis of Interaction

4) Groups

   a) Types of Groups

   b) Group Dynamics

5) Organizations

   a) Types of Organizations

   b) Bureaucracies

   c) The Corporation

6) Interaction, Groups, and Organizations in the Twenty-First Century

7) Looking Ahead

Types of Social Interaction

- Exchange
- Cooperation
- Competition
- Conflict
- Coercion

Components of Interaction

- Status set
- Ascribed status
- Achieved status
- Master status

- Role
- Role conflict
- Role stress
- Role strain

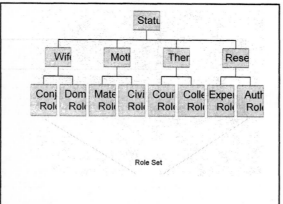

Sociological Analysis of Interaction

- The Dramaturgical Approach
  - Impression management
- Ethnomethodology
  - The methodology for studying the common understanding of everyday life
- Exchange Theory
  - Norm of reciprocity

Groups

- Groups are collections of people who take each other into account as they interact, and who develop a sense of togetherness.
  - Primary groups
  - Secondary groups
  - Reference groups
  - In-groups and out-groups

Group Dynamics

- Leadership
  - Types of leadership
    - Authoritarian
    - Democratic
    - Laissez-faire
  - Group cohesiveness
  - Group conformity

Organizations

- Types of organizations
  - Voluntary
  - Utilitarian
  - Coercive

Bureaucracies: Weber's Analysis

- An ideal type of bureaucracy would have the following characteristics:
  - Complex division of labor
  - A hierarchy of authority
  - Explicit rules and procedures
  - A system that rewards people on the basis of performance
  - Extensive written records

The Negative Consequences of Bureaucracy

- "service without a smile"
- "rules are rules"
- "goal displacement"
- "work expands to fill the time available"
- "bureaucrats rise to the level of incompetence"
- "iron law of oligarchy"
- "invisible woman"

Chapter 7 – Inequalities of Social Class

Social Stratification

- Arrangement of society into layers or strata
- Layers, called castes or classes, are based upon unequal distributions of resources
  - Typical divisions are based upon wealth, power, and prestige

Caste and Class

- Caste systems
  - Fixed social position determined at birth
  - Normally maintained over time by marriage
  - Caste boundaries are maintained by ritual avoidance
  - Challenged by modern ideas and urbanization

- Class systems
  - Social standing determined by factors people can control
    - Educational attainment
    - Income
    - Work experience
  - Class position can change over time

What Determines Social Class?

- Status Consistency: having a similar ranking in three key dimensions
  - Education
    - Helps to raise income
  - Wealth
    - Assets and income influence social standing
  - Occupation and Prestige
    - Prestigious occupations usually require special abilities and long training

38

Occupations of High and Low Prestige

TEN OCCUPATIONS WITH HIGH PRESTIGE	TEN OCCUPATIONS WITH LOW PRESTIGE
1. Physician (86)	1. Barber/Hairdresser (36)
2. Lawyer (75)	2. Construction laborer (36)
3. College professor (74)	3. Truck driver (30)
4. Computer analyst (74)	4. Taxicab driver (28)
5. Architect (73)	5. Waiter/Waitress (28)
6. Dentist (72)	6. Garbage collector (28)
7. Chief executive (70)	7. Gas station attendant (27)
8. Clergy (69)	8. Bill collector (24)
9. Laboratory technologist (68)	9. Janitor (22)
10. High school teacher (66)	10. Messenger (22)

SOURCE: Courtesy of NORC, Chicago, IL, 1994.

American Social Classes

- Upper classes
  - Upper-upper: traditional wealthy elite
  - Lower-upper: recent wealth
- Middle classes
  - Upper-middle: educated professionals
  - Lower-middle: white collar workers; service
- Lower classes
  - Working class: blue collar workers; trades
  - Lower-lower: working poor, chronic poor

Social Mobility in the U.S.

- Intergenerational mobility
  - Mobility of children compared to parents
  - Despite the myths, mobility is similar to other industrial countries
- Structural mobility
  - Movement of categories of people
- Ideology
  - Ideas that legitimize certain social arrangements

The Relationship Between Economic Structure and Ideational Superstructure (Ideology) in Marxian Theory: Ideology and Exploitation

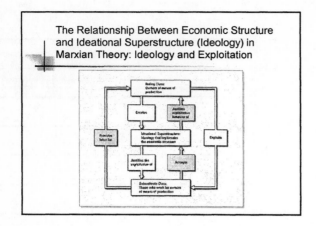

Poverty in the United States

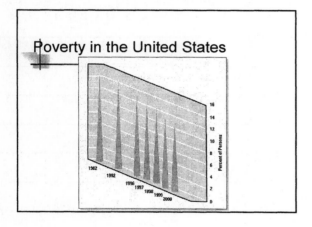

What Is Poverty?

- Relative poverty
  - Poverty by comparison
  - Poor people are those at the bottom
  - Implies that poverty is a permanent feature
- Absolute poverty
  - Those who cannot reach a minimum standard
  - Standards include adequate food, acceptable housing, sufficient clothing

Explaining Poverty

- Culture of poverty
  - Poor have a set of norms and values different from non-poor
  - These ideas keep them from success
  - Children learn from parents and maintain cycle

- Structural poverty
  - Blaming the poor for their own poverty is inaccurate
  - Social arrangements created by wealthier classes work against upward mobility of poor

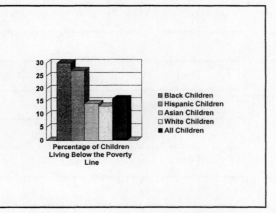

Percentage of Children Living Below the Poverty Line

- ▨ Black Children
- ▨ Hispanic Children
- ▨ Asian Children
- ☐ White Children
- ■ All Children

Stratification: The Functionalist Perspective

- All social positions must be filled
- Each varies in wealth, power, prestige
- Individuals are rewarded
- Positions are filled by those qualified

- Poverty produces benefits
- Are societal rewards fair or not?
- Do rewards actually motivate?
- Are social opportunities equal?

Stratification:
The Conflict Perspective

- Marx: conflict between owners and workers
- Class consciousness will lead to revolution and equality
- But, working class decreased as middle class increased

- Modern day theorists are refining ideas
- Struggle over manipulation of symbols of capital
  - Economic capital
  - Social capital
  - Cultural capital
  - Symbolic capital

Distributive Systems: Lenski

- Societal Resources
  - Necessities
    - Food, shelter
    - Must be shared for social survivability
  - Surplus
    - When attained, not likely to be shared
    - Rigid stratification systems are built
  - Industrial societies
    - Due to enormous production many may share surplus
    - Inequality can decline

Stratification and Symbolic Interactionism

- Inequality is maintained through shared definitions
  - Children are taught to accept inequality
    - Grades as a measure of superiority
  - People learn to accept their inferiority as valid
    - Self fulfilling consequences verified
  - Stereotypes reinforce inequality
    - False perception of poverty and welfare created

Comparison of Three Theoretical Perspectives on Stratification and Class

PERSPECTIVE[a]	VIEW OF STRATIFICATION	KEY CONCEPTS AND PROCESSES
Functionalism	Sees stratification as necessary for efficient operation of society	Social positions Functions Prestige and rewards
Conflict Theory	Sees stratification as a process of exploitation and dominance	Bourgeoisie Proletariat Economic, social, cultural, and symbolic capital
Symbolic Interaction	Sees stratification as created and sustained through social interaction and shared meanings	Informal and formal socialization Self-definitions Stereotypes

CONCEPT WEB Social Inequality

Chapter 8 – Inequalities of Race and Ethnicity

1) Chapter Preview

2) The Great Social Transformation and Racial and Ethnic Inequality

3) Race and Ethnicity

   a) Race

   b) Ethnicity

   c) Minority

4) Prejudice and Discrimination

   a) Stereotypes

   b) Institutional Racism

5) Patterns of Racial and Ethnic Interaction

   a) Assimilation

   b) Pluralism

   c) Expulsion and Annihilation

6) Racial and Ethnic Groups in the United States

   a) White Americans

   b) Native Americans

   c) African Americans

   d) Hispanic Americans

   e) Asian Americans

7) Sociological Analysis of Racial and Ethnic Inequality

   a) The Functionalist Perspective

   b) The Conflict Perspective

   c) The Symbolic Interactionist Perspective

8) Racial and Ethnic Relations in the Twenty-First Century

9) Looking Ahead

Race and Ethnicity

- Race
  - A group of people who are labeled based on physical features
  - These features are arbitrary; no pure races exist
  - Race is a social construct
- Ethnicity
  - A group of people who share common cultural characteristics
  - These characteristics may include language, place of origin, norms and values
  - Race and ethnicity sometimes overlap

Prejudice and Discrimination

- Prejudice
  - An attitude that predisposes an individual to prejudge an entire category of people
  - The prejudice is rigid, emotional rather than logical, and resistant to change
- Discrimination
  - The unfair and harmful treatment of people based upon a group membership
  - May include bias in hiring, promoting, and obtaining membership in social groups
  - Is separate from prejudice; prejudiced people may or may not discriminate

Patterns of Prejudice and Discrimination

	Does Not Discriminate	Discriminates
Unprejudiced	1. Unprejudiced Nondiscriminator. (All-weather Liberal)	2. Unprejudiced discriminator. (Fair-weather Liberal)
Prejudiced	3. Prejudiced Nondiscriminator. (Timid Bigot)	4. Prejudiced Discriminator. (All-weather Bigot)

Stereotypes

- Rigid and inaccurate images that summarize a belief
  - Members of a group are all "stingy" or "clannish"
- Have limited facts, so are self-serving
  - The same characteristics may be interpreted differently depending upon the group
- They persist
  - One group may be elevated over another
  - Stereotypes simplify thinking
  - People have limited knowledge about a group

Racial and Ethnic Interaction

- Assimilation
  - Blending of the culture and structure of one group into society
  - Cultural assimilation: adopting dominant culture as primary culture
  - Structural assimilation: interaction primarily within own group or not
- Pluralism
  - Ethnic groups maintain distinctiveness
  - Ethnic revival: demand for autonomy or independence
  - Symbolic ethnicity: younger generations attempt to preserve ethnic culture

Expulsion and Annihilation

- Expulsion
  - The forceful exclusion of a racial or ethnic group from a society
  - One group needs sufficient power to do it.
  - Examples include Native American relocation
- Annihilation
  - The process by which one group exterminates another
  - Groups could be ethnic, racial, religious, or other
  - Examples include the Nazi extermination of Jews

46

White Americans

- WASP: white, Anglo-Saxon Protestant
  - Most powerful group
  - Original settlers; mostly northern European
- White Ethnics
  - People from other European regions
  - Most came during period of industrialization
  - Groups vary in degree of assimilation

Native Americans

- Original settlers in U.S.
  - Number unknown but perhaps 40 million
- Tribes
  - Originally some 500; now about 170
- Government policies
  - Separation: territories were treated as nations
  - Expulsion: Indian removal, including extermination, to western regions
  - Forced assimilation: after 1880
    - Americanizing and dissolution of Indian culture
    - After 1930, tribal restoration

Largest Native American Tribes

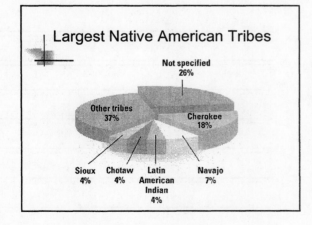

African Americans

- Slavery period: settlement to 1865
  - Original culture lost
- Reconstruction to post-WW2
  - Emancipation and conflict
  - Legal segregation: "Jim Crow" laws
- Contemporary period
  - Civil rights movement
    - Brown v. Board of Education
    - Black Pride and revitalization of African American culture
  - Continuing struggle with race and class

Hispanic Americans/Latinos

- Mexican Americans
  - Soon to become the largest ethnic minority
  - Catholic; strong family ties
  - Settlement in southwest perpetuates native culture
- Puerto Rican Americans
  - Citizens of U.S. (Commonwealth status)
  - Settlement in northeast
- Cuban Americans
  - Major immigration since 1959
  - Settlement in Florida

Asian Americans

- Chinese Americans
  - Early immigrants: mines and railroads
  - Hostility led to urban enclaves
- Japanese Americans
  - Early immigrants soon turned to farming
  - War relocation and ultimate compensation
- Recent Groups
  - Refugees
  - New immigration policies

The Chances: 1990-2000					
	WHITE	BLACK	HISPANIC	ASIAN	NATIVE AMERICAN
Education: % with college degree	26	15	11	44	9
Poverty: % below poverty line	9	22	21	14	31
Births: % low birth weight	6	13	6	7	7
Death Rate per 1,000 (age adjusted)	453	1,225	NA	502	699

SOURCE: U.S. Bureau of the Census 1994, 1996, 1992.

Comparison of Three Theoretical Perspectives on Race and Ethnicity		
PERSPECTIVE[a]	VIEW OF RACIAL AND ETHNIC INEQUALITY	KEY CONCEPTS AND PROCESSES
Functionalism	Sees inequality as beneficial to society because it ensures that unpleasant work gets done	Functions (positive consequences) Job allocation a matter of matching skills to existing opportunities
Conflict Theory	Sees inequality as a process of exploitation and dominance	Competition Conflict for scarce resources
Symbolic Interaction	Sees race and ethnicity as created and sustained through social interaction and shared meanings	Consciousness of kind Identity

---

CONCEPT WEB Racial and Ethnic Inequality

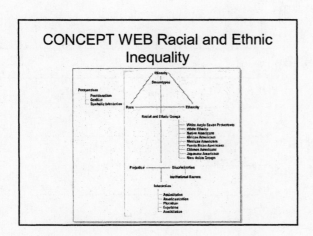

Chapter 9 – Inequalities of Gender

1) Chapter Preview

2) The Great Social Transformation and Gender Inequality

3) Gender-Role Socialization

   a) Socialization and Gender

   b) Agents of Gender Socialization

   c) Age and Gender-Role Socialization

4) Patriarchy and Everyday Life

   a) Language and Patriarchy

   b) Social Interaction and Patriarchy

5) Gender Inequality and Work

   a) Working Women

   b) Work Segregation

   c) Income Inequality

6) Feminism

   a) Gender Equality and the Law

   b) Comparable Worth

   c) Abortion

   d) Resistant to Compulsory Heterosexism

   e) Inclusive Feminism

6) Sociological Analysis of Gender Inequality

   a) The Functionalist Perspective

   b) The Conflict Perspective

   c) The Symbolic Interactionist Perspective

7) Gender Inequality in the Twenty-First Century

8) Looking Ahead

Inequalities of Gender

- Sexual harassment
  - Unwanted sexual attention or pressure from someone of greater power
- Patriarchy
  - Social arrangement where men dominate women
- Sexism
  - Ideology maintaining women are inferior to men, justifying discrimination

Gender Socialization:
Learning the Cultural and Attitudinal Qualities
Associated with Males and Females

- Gender role
  - What does society expect from a male or a female
    - Social meanings attached to biological qualities vary from society to society
- Gender markers
  - Symbols and signs that identify gender
    - Examples include choice of appropriate colors or naming patterns

Agents of Gender Socialization

- Living space
  - Designs and artifacts in boys/girls rooms
- Play
  - Encouraging different roles through toys
- Dress
  - Clothing styles affect behavior
- School
  - Reading materials contain gender stereotypes
- Advertising
  - Biased images exaggerated to sell product

Patriarchy and Everyday Life

- Language
  - Slang degrades women
  - Honorific titles or first name
  - Choice of words appropriate to gender
  - Marriage name changing
- Social interaction
  - Physical domination by men when interacting
  - Men interrupt women more often
  - Bias in "polite behavior"

Gender Inequality and Work

- Working women
  - Increased participation of women in all aspects of labor force is a recent change
- Work segregation
  - Certain job categories (clerical and service) still dominated by women
  - Second shift: still strong household obligations
- Income inequality
  - Women, on average, earn less than men

Causes of Gender Inequality in the Workplace

- Sexism
  - Women are best suited for certain jobs or should stay at home
- Lack of qualifications
  - Men have greater experience
- The Glass Ceiling
  - Difficulties for women to rise to top positions
- Networking
  - "old boy" network excludes women

Feminist Issues

- Legal equality
  - Battling obstacles to equal protection
- Comparable worth
  - Equal pay for comparable jobs
- Abortion
  - Men should not dominate choice
- Resistance to compulsory heterosexism
  - Freedom to choose sexual orientation
- Inclusive feminism
  - Traditional definitions of inequality – race and class – should include gender

Gender: Theoretical Perspectives

- Functionalism
  - Is gender inequality functional for society?
    - Division of labor maintains family
- Conflict
  - Men will subordinate women
    - New ideology will eliminate false consciousness
- Symbolic interactionism
  - Symbols and images reinforce stereotypes

Comparison of Three Theoretical Perspectives on Gender Inequality

PERSPECTIVE[a]	VIEW OF GENDER INEQUALITY	KEY CONCEPTS AND PROCESSES
Functionalism	Sees gender inequality as an orderly mechanism for dividing labor and allocating rewards	Expressive tasks Instrumental tasks
Conflict Theory	Sees gender inequality as a form of social stratification in which men dominate women	Subordination False consciousness
Symbolic Interaction	Sees gender inequality as transmitted from generation to generation through gender-role socialization	Gender stereotypes Self-definitions

53

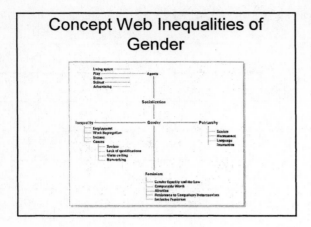

Concept Web Inequalities of Gender

Chapter 10 – The Economy

Sociology and the Economy

- Economy
  - The social institution that determines production and distribution of goods and services
- Capitalism
  - Free-Market competition determines production and distribution
  - Private ownership
  - Pursuit of profit
- Socialism
  - Means of production publicly owned
  - State directs production and distribution

Capitalism

- Free market competition
  - Laissez-fair: no government interference in economy
- Private ownership
  - A right without government obstacles
- Pursuit of profit
  - Greatest good for people results
  - Critique: heartless, cyclical, ignores poor, long term social harm

Socialism

- Public ownership desirable
  - Everyone should share equally in products and goods
  - Key resources and services protected
  - Private ownership increases inequality
- Critique: inefficiency and overregulation

Mixed Economies: A Blend

- Both capitalist and socialist economies can face similar problems
  - New technology, labor issues, demographic changes require similar adjustments
- Social insurance
  - Government must maintain minimum social standards

Corporate Power

- Major shareholders and company officers dominate policymaking
  - Most shareholders do not participate
- Interlocking directorate
  - Multiple board membership link different companies
- Conglomerates
  - Giant corporation composed of other corporations

The Multinational Corporation:

- Companies that conduct business in several countries but have their central headquarters in one country
- Problems of power and control
  - Many different laws
- Vast assets
  - Can influence local host countries
- Most benefits to corporation
  - Host countries get jobs, training

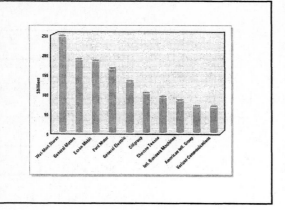

Unemployment

- People without jobs seeking work
  - Some groups are not seeking work or can not work
- Closely watched economic indicator
  - Rate change affects millions
- Zero rate unobtainable
  - Some unemployment inevitable
- Acceptable level of unemployment
  - 5% generally acceptable in U.S.
- Social stigma
  - Dependent status with limited options, help

Job Loss Anxiety:
Workers suffer over perceived insecurity

- Economic shifts, downsizing, greed lead to job losses
  - Fairness of the system challenged
- Workers have real fears
  - About 10% of workforce worry
- Many negative consequences
  - Loss of money, confidence, faith in society
- Fundamental flaw in capitalism
  - "Marketplace" offers few protections

Economy: Functionalist Perspective

- Capitalism encourages the economic system
  - Free markets and profits encourages production and distribution of goods and services
- Cooperation in economics and politics
  - Wealth and power lead to new businesses
- Innovation
  - Competition leads to adaptation

Economy: Conflict Perspective

- Economy is unstable and doomed
  - Free market produces class conflict and worker alienation
- Vast inequalities
  - Unequal distribution of wealth perpetuated by powerful
- Ideology supports capitalism
  - Winners have right to wealth; losers blame themselves

The Economy and the Future

- Deindustrialization
  - Service jobs replacing manufacturing jobs
  - Many will be low paid creating a "two tiered" workforce
- Women in the labor force
  - Women entering male dominated occupations
  - Breaking through more layers of glass ceiling
  - Family size and dynamics effected

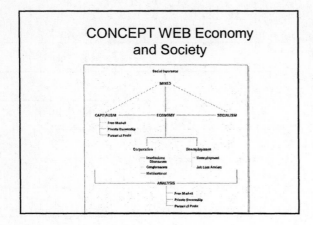

Chapter 11 – The Political Order

1) Chapter Preview

2) The Great Social Transformation and the Political Order

3) Power and the Political Order

   a) Traditional Authority

   b) Legal-Rational Authority

   c) Charismatic Authority

4) The State and the Exercise of Power

   a) Types of States

   b) Nations and States

   c) War and Terrorism

   d) Terrorism

   e) States and Human Rights

5) Political Processes in the United States

   a) Political Parties

   b) Special-Interest Groups

   c) Voting

6) Power-Elite and Pluralist Models

   a) The Power-Elite Model

   b) The Pluralist Model

7) Sociological Analysis of the Political Order

   a) The Functionalist Perspective

   b) The Conflict Perspective

   c) The Symbolic Interactionist Perspective

8) The Political Order in the Twenty-First Century

9) Looking Ahead

Power and the Political Order

- Power
  - the ability to achieve ends despite resistance
- Illegitimate power
  - Society does not approve of the way that power is applied
  - This type of power is called coercion
- Legitimate power
  - Society approves of the way that power is applied
  - This type of power is called authority

Types of Authority

- Traditional
  - Authority is legitimized by the historical beliefs and practices of a society
  - Kings rule according to tradition
- Legal-rational
  - Authority is derived from rules and laws
  - Rules are written in constitutions or charters
- Charismatic
  - Authority is derived from an individual's exceptional personal qualities
  - Qualities include personal magnetism or wisdom

Exercising Power

- Ideal types
  - An abstract description that reveals the essential features
  - Types of authority are ideals
- State
  - The highest political authority within a territory
- Government
  - The people who are directing the state

Types of States

- Authoritarian
  - People are excluded from governing process
  - Opposition not usually permitted
  - Government is not interested in daily life of the people
- Totalitarian
  - Government has unlimited power
  - Tolerates no opposition
  - Close control over activities of citizens
- Democratic
  - Allows citizen input in governing
  - Permits elections and dismissing of leaders

Nations and States

- State
  - The highest political authority in an area
- Nation
  - A group that lives within a territory and shares a common history, culture and identity
- Nation-state
  - The supreme political authority within a territory that incorporates a nation
  - A combination of nation and state

War: An institutionalized violent conflict between nations or tribes

- Total war
  - An instrument of foreign policy
  - Every resource must be devoted to victory
- Marx
  - Seeds in capitalism: never ending need for resources
- Institutional theory
  - Cooperative relations between institutions
    - Military industrial complex dominates foreign policy
    - United Nations can confer legitimacy

Terrorism:

A non-institutionalized use of threat, intimidation, and violence to reach a political objective.

- Terrorists can use any methods
  - No institutionalized support or authority
- Intent is to spread fear, discontent, and panic
  - Selected targets: special category of people
  - Random targets: anyone at any time
- Eventually, people insist government must agree to terrorist demands
  - Exchange for ending violence

Human Rights

- Broadly defined rights people are entitled by virtue their humanity
  - Includes freedom and equality
- Amnesty International
  - Voluntary organization publicly monitors violations
  - No effective international organization can prevent human rights violations

Political Parties

- A political organization meant to legitimately influence the government
- A two-party system in the U.S. keeps third parties ineffective

- Parties can influence government appointments
- Parties form coalitions for united stands
- Parties are focus for conflict
  - Party platform defines ideology, goals, and differences from opposing party

Special Interest Groups

- Lobbyists
  - A person employed by a corporation, union, or other organization
  - Intent is to influence congressional votes on certain bills
- Interest group
  - An organization formed to sway political decisions
- PAC
  - Political Action Committees raise money for special interest groups

Voting: The opportunity to elect government officials.

- Voter participation
  - Many do not vote in U.S.
  - High rates of voting in Europe
- Voting and social groups
  - Poor and minorities less likely to vote
  - Gender differences reflect differing concerns
- Voter registration
  - Requirements may discourage participation

Power Elite

- Small group controls the U.S.
  - Economy, Government, Military
- Social elites
  - Know each other
  - Share a similar world view
  - Work cooperatively to achieve a political agenda

Pluralist Model

- Power is diffused throughout society
  - Multiple centers of power
    - Business associations, Unions, Schools
    - Ethnic groups
  - Veto groups
    - Power centers that are able to block actions of other groups
      - Multinational corporations, professional organizations

Politics and Functionalism

- Maintaining order
  - A major social function
  - State must assume this responsibility
- Interact with other states
  - Treaties and alliances must be accomplished through a central authority
- Direct the system
  - state must be responsible for regulating important institutions and procedures

Conflict and the Political Order

- Conflict is an inherent part of the political order
  - Various groups must compete for limited resources
  - Struggle for outcomes depend on wealth and power
- Democracy does not prevent power from being centralized in hands of few
  - Tools of democracy don't always work

Symbolic Interaction

- Political socialization
  - Formal and informal learning that creates a political self identity
- Agents
  - Families create initial political attitudes
  - Media creates powerful images and information

_____

_____

_____

_____

_____

_____

_____

CONCEPT WEB The Political Order

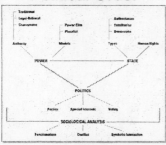

_____

_____

_____

_____

_____

_____

_____

Chapter 12 – Marriage and Family

1) Chapter Preview

2) The Great Social Transformation and Marriage and the Family

3) Types of Families

4) Marriage and Kinship

    a) Kinship Patterns

    b) Marriage

    c) Romantic Love

    d) Courtship

    e) Dimensions of Marriage and Family

5) Alternative Family Forms in the United States

    a) Serial Monogamy

    b) The Single-Parent Family

    c) Gay and Lesbian Families

    d) Cohabitation

    e) Independent Living

6) Racial and Ethnic Variations in Family Forms

    a) The African American Family

    b) The Mexican American Family

7) Issues in Marriage and Family

    a) Marital Dissolution

    b) Explaining Marital Dissolution

    c) Domestic Violence

8) Sociological Analysis of Marriage and Family

    a) The Functionalist Perspective

    b) The Conflict Perspective

    c) The Symbolic Interactionist Perspective

9) Marriage and Family in the Twenty-First Century

10) Looking Ahead

What Is a Family?

- A social unit of some number of people who are linked intimately
  - Related in some way
  - Usually living together
  - Engaging in sex
  - Having responsibility for rearing children
  - Functioning as an economic unit

Types of Families

- **Nuclear Family**: a social unit composed of a husband, a wife, and their children
  - Family of orientation: family to which one was born
  - Family of procreation: a person, spouse, and their children
  - Blended family: spouses and their children from former marriages live as a single nuclear family
  - Binuclear family: divorced parents form separate households; children divide their time with each

- **Extended Family**
  - Composed of two or more generations of kin that functions as an independent social and economic unit

Kinship Patterns

- A network of people who are related by marriage, blood, or social practice
  - Kinship is a means by which societies can socialize children and transmit culture from one generation to the next
  - Kinship creates complex social bonds
    - Aff inal relationships are social bonds based on marriage

Marriage

- Two individuals involved in a socially approved relationship
  - Intimate, mutual long-term obligations
  - Fulfilled customary ceremonial or legal requirements

Romantic Love

- An emotional identification between two individuals
  - Intense
  - Convinced they cannot live without each other
- Not considered important for marriage until 20th century
  - An important incentive to marry
  - Love provides a source of support
  - Strong commitment to each other

Courtship

- The relationship between two people who are preparing for marriage to each other
  - Endogamy: people marry within their own group
  - Exogamy: people marry outside of their own group
  - Propinquity: people meet only when they are not apart
  - Ethnicity and race: people tend to marry within their own groups
  - Values: endogamy is reinforced by cultural values

Dimensions of Marriage and Family

- Number of spouses
  - Monogamy: one male spouse, one female spouse
  - Polygamy: multiple spouses
    - Polygyny multiple wives
    - Polyandry: multiple husbands
    - Groups marriage: multiple spouses

Dimensions of Marriage and Family

- Residence
  - Norms related to where married couples should reside
    - Matrilocal arrangement: kin lives with wife's mother
    - Patrilocal arrangement: kin lives with husband's mother
    - Neolocal arrangement: kin set up independent household
    - Bilocal arrangement: each spouse maintains a separate residence

Dimensions of Marriage and Family

- Descent
  - The system by which kinship is traced over generations
    - Patrilineal: kinship is traced through male
    - Matrilineal: kinship is traced through female
    - Bilineal: kinship is traced through both sides of the family

- Power
  - The system by which power is assigned
    - Patriarchy: male has most power
    - Matriarchy: female has most power
      - Matricentric: females have some power

Alternative Family Forms

- Serial monogamy
  - More than one spouse but not at same time
- Single parent
  - Mostly result of divorce
- Gay and lesbian
  - Legal issues debated
- Cohabitation
  - A household without marriage
- Independent living
  - Men or women who live alone

_____
_____
_____
_____
_____
_____
_____

The Mexican American Family

- Strong family values
  - Family has priority over individual
  - Extended families maintained
- Patriarchy
  - Machismo: a value system embracing highly masculine behaviors including a double standard
- Authoritarian child rearing
  - Father has final disciplinary authority
- Influences of American culture
  - Patriarchy and extended family decline

_____
_____
_____
_____
_____
_____
_____

Marital Dissolution

- Divorce
  - Dissolution of legal ties that bind a marriage
  - Legal separation
    - Couples agree to take up separate residences
    - Informal separation: one spouse temporarily moves out
  - Desertion
    - One spouse leaves the other for a prolonged period of time

_____
_____
_____
_____
_____
_____
_____

Explaining Marital Dissolution

- Society
  - Nuclear family is subject to many stresses but has limited resources
  - Lower social classes more vulnerable
- Falling out of love
  - Passion yields to reality
- Women's changing roles
  - Less economic dependency

Domestic Violence

- Amount
  - 1/5 of women abused
- Class differences
  - Type of violence and reporting patterns
- Stay or leave?
  - Retribution and psychological dependence
- Options
  - Shelters and legal system
- Global patterns
  - National tolerance level
  - Stress from rapid social change

Functionalism and the Family
The Family Satisfies Common Social Functions

- Socialization
  - Family is responsible for primary care and early learning
- Birth; regulates sexual activity
  - Choosing mates and perpetuating population
- Economic
  - Assigning assets
  - Important economic production and consumption unit
- Support and comfort
  - Help with problems
- Social placement
  - Children inherit status and class of parents

Family: Conflict Perspective

- Power relationships
  - Men control wealth
  - Norms require women to do most domestic chores
- Perpetuation of social inequality
  - Family is a model of patriarchy that dominates society

Family: Symbolic Interactionism

- People construct their own families
  - No two families are alike
- Family is source of major roles and identity
  - As new roles are learned
  - New concepts of reality are created

Chapter 13 – Education

1) Chapter Preview

2) The Great Social Transformation and Education

3) Cross-Cultural Comparisons: The United States and Japan

   a) Education in the United States

   b) Education in Japan

4) Education and Inequality

   a) Education and Racial-Ethnic Segregation

   b) Education and Language

   c) Education, Testing, and Inequality

   d) Education and Gender

   e) Education and Tracking

5) Changing the Educational System

   a) Magnet Schools

   b) Charter Schools

   c) Freedom of Choice

   d) No Child Left Behind

   e) Homeschooling

6) Sociological Analysis of Education

   a) The Functionalist Perspective

   b) The Conflict Perspective

   c) The Symbolic Interactionist Perspective

7) Education in the Twenty-First Century

8) Looking Ahead

Sociology and Education

- Education
  - Transferal of the knowledge, values, and beliefs of a society from one generation to the next
- Formal education
  - Transmission of knowledge, skills, and attitudes from one generation to the next through systematic training
- Schools
  - Places of formal educational instruction

Education in the U.S.

- Decentralized control
  - Local and independent schools
- Mass education
  - Education is essential for democracy
  - Industrialization required expanded knowledge
- Practicality
  - Education must be relevant to people's lives
- Credentialism
  - Skills and knowledge validated
  - Educational inflation: overeducated for a job

Education in Japan

- Conformity, selectivity, standardization
  - Schools must prepare students to properly fit into society
- Effort is key to success
  - People have similar abilities
  - Strong family obligation to learning
- Serious schooling
  - Hard work, long hours, juku
  - Limited other life choices
- National exams lead to placement
  - Thorough education for vast majority
  - Low scores produce shame

Education and Inequality

- Education and Racial-Ethnic Segregation
  - 1954 Supreme Court decision
  - "Neighborhood Schools"
  - Busing
  - White flight
- Education and Language
- Education, Testing, and Inequality
  - SAT and ACT
- Education and Gender
- Education and Tracking

Mandatory Busing

- Court ordered desegregation
  - 1954 Supreme Court decision
- White flight and backlash
  - School segregation persists
  - Poor minorities schools deteriorate
- Race or class?
  - Neighborhood schools preferred
- Magnet schools
  - Alternative offers specialized curriculum available to all

Language Instruction

- What language will be used for teaching?
  - English is traditionally used for mainstream students
- Large immigration population
  - Native language instruction
    - Costly where many different languages spoken
    - Encourages social isolation
  - Mainstream language immersion
    - Encourage English language abilities quickly

Testing

- Standardized placement tests
  - Test bias
    - Minorities' scores are different from whites'
    - Cultural and social class experiences differ
- Cultural literacy
  - People should have the basic information to thrive in modern world
    - Common culture and curriculum should be created
- Multiculturalists advocate educational diversity
  - Curriculum should reflect diversity

Gender Bias

- Education: individual achievement
  - Interpreted differently for males and females
    - Domestic roles taught for females
    - Academic emphasis for males
  - Today, more opportunities for women
    - Non-sexist attitudes promoted
    - Gender discrimination illegal

Schools and "Choice"

- Right to attend school of choice with public support
  - Public schools are "failing"
  - Vouchers for private schools
  - Religious schools could receive public funding
  - Curriculum can vary
- Taxpayers fund public schools
  - Freedom to choose schools exists already
  - "choice" threat to neighborhood, community, and public schools
  - Loss of curriculum consistency
  - Decline of educational standards

No Child Left Behind

- NCLB Act passed by Congress in 2001
- Requires annual testing
- Satisfactory attainment
- Sanctions
- Opponents
  - Teaching to the test
  - Greater inequality among schools

Schools and Functionalism

- The educational institution provides important social functions
  - Socialization
    - Formal learning in schools
    - Hidden curriculum teaches important values
  - Integration into society
    - Schools help assimilate newcomers
  - Social placement
    - Schools sort people according to ability
    - Ability leads to placement in social positions

Schools and the Conflict Perspective

- Educational system perpetuates social inequality
  - Success defined by wealthy and powerful
    - Working class and poor have disadvantage
  - Access to private, prestigious schools limited
    - Exceptional educational opportunities are not available to non-wealthy
    - Perpetuates inequality
  - Structural arrangements perpetuate inequality
    - Tracking: social class bias limits future opportunities

Symbolic Interaction and Schools

- The school influences social roles and development of self
  - Teacher definitions
    - Student labeling creates a "self-fulfilling prophecy"
      - "Good learners" gain confidence
      - "Poor learners" failures reinforced
    - May effect ultimate career choices
  - Other shared definitions
    - attitudes may be shaped by cultural diversity

CONCEPT WEB Education

Chapter 14 – Religion

Religion and Society

- A system of beliefs, rituals, and ceremonies
- Focus is on sacred matters
- Promotes community among followers
- Provides a personal spiritual experience for its members

The Great Transformation

- In communal societies, religion permeated all aspects of society.
- In contemporary industrial society, the institution of religion has become separated from many social and economic activities
- Max Weber
  - *The Protestant Ethic and the Spirit of Capitalism*

Characteristics of Religion

- Beliefs
  - Ideas, based upon faith, that people consider true
- The sacred and profane
  - Sacred: that which has supernatural qualities
  - Profane: that which is the ordinary
- Rituals
  - Routines that reinforce the faith
- Moral communities
  - People who share a religious belief
- Personal experience
  - Grants meaning to life

Religious Organization

- Church
  - A formal religious group well established and integrated into society
- Ecclesia
  - a system by which a religion becomes the official religion of a state
- Denomination
  - A religion that maintains friendly relations with the government but does not claim to be the only legitimate religion

Sects and Cults

- Sects:
  - Loosely organized religious group
  - Non professional leadership
  - Actively rejects social environment
  - Breaks away from a larger religious group
- Cults
  - Non-conventional religious group
  - Social conditions demand separation
  - Members required to withdraw from normal life
  - Full-time communal obligation for members

Christianity

- World's largest religion
- Three main branches
  - Roman Catholic
  - Protestant
    - Luther breaks away from Roman Catholic Church in 16th century
  - Orthodox Christian
    - Division of Christianity in 10th century
    - Serves eastern Europe

Islam

- Second largest religion in world
- Significant beliefs and practices
  - Only one god that all must recognize
  - Daily prayer, share wealth, pilgrimage
- No centralized authority
  - Local clerics rule often with close state ties
  - Two major sects
    - Sunni
    - Shiite

Judaism

- Numerically smallest of world religions
- Important beliefs:
  - God's chosen people
  - Torah: first 5 books of the Bible; oldest truths from God
- Major divisions
  - Orthodox: strictly traditional
  - Reform: liberal and worldly
  - Conservative: middle ground between Orthodox and Reform

Hinduism

- Largest of the Eastern religions
  - Concentrated largely in India
- Important beliefs
  - Dharma: special force makes daily demands and sacred obligations
  - Karma: spirit remains through life, death, rebirth
- Organization
  - Caste membership

Buddhism

- Large religion throughout Asia
  - Includes southeast Asian countries and China
- Based upon teachings of the Buddha, the enlightened one
  - Monks and lay people spread his teachings
- Important beliefs
  - To relieve human suffering one must follow a path that ultimately leads to enlightenment
  - "Right" thoughts and actions must be daily performed and evaluated through meditation

Confucianism

- Originated with Confucius attempting to solve practical problems of daily living
  - Wisdom summarized guides management of society
    - Jen: human sympathy that binds people in 5 basic relationships
      - Sovereign and subject
      - Parent and child
      - Older brother and younger brother
      - Husband and wife
      - Friend and friend
    - Proper etiquette and ritual help these relationships

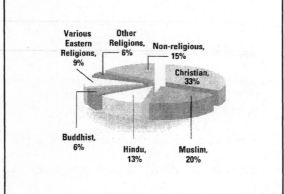

Religion and Functionalism

- Religion, as a major social institution, provides many important functions
  - Cohesion
    - Reduce social isolation
    - Increase social solidarity
  - Social control
    - Authority over significant events
    - Social violations become moral offenses
  - Purpose
    - Reduction of anxiety regarding the unknown

Conflict Perspective and Religion

- Religion is a tool of the ruling class
  - Focus on "otherworldly matters" detracts from this world concerns
    - Passive acceptance of misery
    - True rewards will come in afterlife
  - Inequality and domination is legitimate
    - A false consciousness is created
- Liberation theologist critique
  - Religion can be a powerful agent of social change
    - Counter ruling class power

Symbolic Interaction and Religion

- The creation of a social identity
  - A religious identity is a main element is certain social interactions
  - Others who keep religion private still find it creates an important part of their personal identity
  - Radical religious changes may lead to a fundamental shift in identity
- Important agents of religious socialization
  - Family: earliest religious learning
  - Schools: separation of church and state issues

Secularization

- The declining influence of religion in daily life
  - Combines with increasing influence of science
- Religious groups see social decline
  - Problems can be solved through renewed religious influences

Civil Religion

- The quasi-religious beliefs that link people to society and country
  - Countries confer sacredness upon non-religious aspects of life
    - Patriotism ceremonies
  - Crimes and moral violations are equated
    - "blue laws"
- Civil religion reinforces core values and strengthens communal bonds

Religion Today

- The Megachurch
  - All-inclusive church draws large audiences
  - Several hundred exist in U.S.
  - Largest concentration found in Southwest
  - Approximately half are nondenominational
    - Church becomes daily-life center

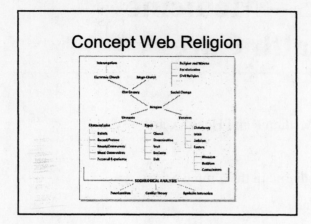

_____

_____

_____

_____

_____

_____

Chapter 15 – Medicine and Health Care

1) Chapter Preview

2) The Great Social Transformation and Medicine and Health Care

3) Health and Society

    a) The Historical Development of Medicine in the United States

    b) The Social Organization of Medicine

    c) Health Care Organizations

4) Sociological Issues in Medicine and Health Care

    a) Inequality in Health and Health Care

    b) The Cost of Health Care

    c) Health Insurance

    d) The Medicalization of Society

5) Sociological Analysis of Medicine and Health Care

    a) The Functionalist Perspective

    b) The Conflict Perspective

    c) The Symbolic Interactionist Perspective

6) Medicine and Health Care in the Twenty-First Century

7) Looking Ahead

Sociology and Medicine

- Epidemic
  - A widespread outbreak of a contagious disease
- Pandemic
  - An outbreak of a contagious disease over a very large area or worldwide
- Disease
  - A pathology that disrupts the usual functions of the body
- Health
  - The capacity to satisfy role requirements

Social Organization of Medicine

- Physicians
  - Have the authority to diagnose, prescribe treatment
  - Certify death or competency
  - Prestige results in many privileges
  - Most are specialists today
- Nurses
  - Assist in medical settings under the supervision of a physician
  - Have less education than physician
  - Most are women

Health Care Organizations

- Hospitals
  - Divided authorities
    - Physicians
    - Administrators
  - Multihospital systems
    - Hospitals managed by a company
- HMO
  - An insurance plan combined with a facility
  - A "health maintenance organization"
    - For a monthly fee, comprehensive health care is provided

Social Issues in Health

- Social class
  - Quality of care varies according to social class
  - Social class is related to a healthy environment
- Race and ethnicity
  - Race and class are connected
- Gender
  - Male physicians less familiar with female health and medicine

Cost of Health Care

- Physician fees
  - Fee for service greatly increased
    - Due to extensive testing, defensive medicine, insurance premiums
- Hospitals
  - Complex facility
  - Often profit driven
- Technology
  - Increased dependence on sophisticated and costly devices

Health Insurance

- 70% have health insurance in U.S.
  - Co-payments common
- Uninsured tend to be:
  - Racial minorities
  - Young people
  - Poor people
- Special insurance
  - Medicare: health insurance for the elderly
  - Medicaid: health care for poor and disabled

Medicalization of Society:
The growing power of medicine as an institution.

- Simple processes have become medically complex
  - birth
- Redefinition of problems as diseases
  - Addictions are medical problems
  - Mental disorders
  - Physical renewal

Functionalist Perspective

- Medicine is functional for society
  - People must be healthy to serve society
  - Sickness must be treated and cured so that society will be able to continue
  - Medicine drives scientific research
  - People must follow social norms related to health
  - Medicine produces great wealth so motivates people to enter those professions

The Sick Role:
Social Control Over Sickness

- Sick people are not responsible for their condition
- Sick people may withdraw from normal activities
- Sick people should want to get well
- Sick people should seek treatment

Conflict Perspective

- Medical cure and care has become big business
  - Costly and expensive
  - Serves country poorly
- System perpetuates inequality
  - Some groups lack access
- Intense competition
  - Produces inefficiency
  - Battles over power

 ## Symbolic Interaction

- Socialization of physicians and nurses
  - Learning to become detached and impersonal
  - Conflict between compassion and bureaucracy
- Physician-patient interaction
  - Misunderstandings are common
- Disease recovery
  - Social context can influence cure

 ## Health Today

- Preventive medicine
  - Lifestyle changes have broad social effect
  - Aging population
  - Global view of health
- Cultural competence
  - Health care must be sensitive to wide range of diverse social conditions

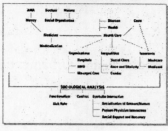

CONCEPT WEB Medicine and Health Care

_____

_____

_____

_____

_____

_____

Chapter 16 – Population, Ecology, and Urbanization

Demographic Analysis

- Population explosion
  - A rapid unchecked growth in the number of people inhabiting an area
- Population implosion
  - A rapid unchecked decline in the number of people inhabiting an area
- Demography
  - The scientific study of the size, growth and composition of the human population
    - Fertility, mortality, migration

Fertility

- Fertility
  - Number of births that occur over a specific period, usually one year
  - Replacement level: number of children required to replace the population as people die
  - Crude birth rate: annual number of births in a population per 1000 members of the population
    - The simplest measure of fertility
  - General fertility ratio: the annual number of births in a population per 1000 women aged 15-44
    - A refined, more accurate fertility measurement

Mortality

- Mortality
  - The number of deaths that occur during a year
- Life expectancy
  - How long people probably will live
- Life span
  - The theoretical maximum length of life
- Crude death rate
  - Annual number of deaths per 1000 members of the population
- Rate of natural increase
  - The number of births in a population exceed the number of deaths
- Rate of natural decrease
  - The number of deaths in a population exceed the number of births

Migration

- The movement of people from one area of residence to another.
  - Immigration
    - The movement of people into a place
  - Emigration
    - The movement of people out of a place
  - Net migration rate
    - The annual difference between those entering and those leaving per 1000 population

Demographic Transition
An explanation of population change

- Stage 1: Preindustrial
  - High birth rate, high death rate
- Stage 2: Early Transitional
  - High birth rate, declining death rate
    - Technology reduces death rate
- Stage 3: Late Transitional
  - Declining birth rate, low death rate
    - Urbanization reduces birth rate
- Stage 4: Industrial
  - Low birth rate, low death rate

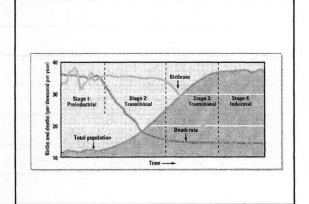

In What Stage of the Demographic Transition Is Each of the Following?

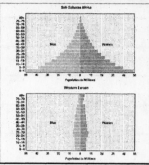

Malthus

- Population growth
  - Can be very rapid
  - Can outdistance food supply
- Population control
  - Positive checks
    - "natural" conditions such as famine, war, disease will reduce population
  - Preventive checks
    - Postpone marriage, sexual abstinence
- Inevitable cyclical changes
  - Nations doomed to alternating periods of prosperity and misery

---

Was Malthus Correct?

- Neo-Malthusians
  - Concern with technological over-reliance
    - Limits to technology are near
  - Disaster is developing now
    - Little reason for women to reduce fertility in poor countries
- Cornucopians
  - Human inventiveness will prevail
  - Green Revolution
    - Technological advances have resulted in more food
    - Earth can support many more people

Human Ecology
The study of the relationship between society and the environment

- POET: how does each factor influence an issue?
  - Population
    - What are the characteristics of the population?
  - Organization
    - How is the system designed to cope?
  - Environment
    - What is the nature of the physical environment?
  - Technology
    - What changes in technology have occurred?

Urbanization:
The increase in the percentage of population residing in cities

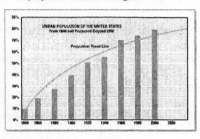

Urbanization in Traditional Societies

- Primate city
  - Dominant city in a nation
    - Magnet for migration
    - When city has 20% of national population, relatives abound
    - Growth of squatter settlements
      - Limited services
    - Housing opportunities must provide essential services
      - Often growth is rapid and chaotic

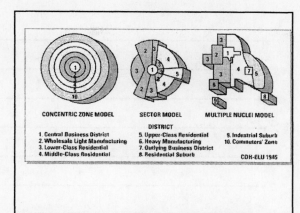

CONCENTRIC ZONE MODEL   SECTOR MODEL   MULTIPLE NUCLEI MODEL

DISTRICT

1. Central Business District
2. Wholesale Light Manufacturing
3. Lower-Class Residential
4. Middle-Class Residential

5. Upper-Class Residential
6. Heavy Manufacturing
7. Outlying Business District
8. Residential Suburb

9. Industrial Suburb
10. Commuters' Zone

CDH-ELU 1945

Urbanization in Industrial Societies

- Concentric zone
  - City grows in "rings"
    - Continuous migration to outer rings
- Sector
  - City grows in uneven regions
    - Major streets, business clusters
- Multiple-nuclei
  - Suburbs become integrated into central city
    - Numerous specialized centers

Urbanism:
The pattern of social life in cities.

- Size
  - Growth leads to diversity
  - Interaction becomes formalized, rational
- Density
  - With growth, interaction becomes transitory and symbolic
  - Congestion produces social pathologies
- Heterogeneity
  - Diversity leads to tolerance

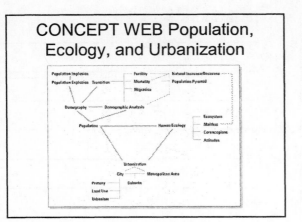

CONCEPT WEB Population, Ecology, and Urbanization

_____

_____

_____

_____

_____

_____

_____

Chapter 17 – Collective Social Action

1) Chapter Preview

2) The Great Social Transformation and Collective Social Action

3) Collective Behavior

   a) Crowds

   b) Riots, Panics, and Rumors

   c) Social Theory and Crowd Behavior

4) Social Movements

   a) Types of Social Movements

   b) Social Theory and Social Movements

5) Social Movements in the United States

   a) The Civil Rights Movement

   b) The Women's Movement

   c) The Environmental Movement

   d) Relations among Social Movements

6) Collective Social Action and Working for Change

   a) Changing Individuals

   b) Changing Organizations

   c) Changing Institutions

   d) Why People Resist Change

7) Collective Social Action in the Twenty-First Century

8) Looking Ahead

Emergence of Collective Behavior

- Structured Conduciveness
  - Preexisting conditions such as rumors
- Structured Strains
  - Degree of popular anxiety
- Generalized Beliefs
  - Can anything be done to solve a problem?
- Precipitating Factors
  - Spontaneous event that precipitates action
- Mobilization for Action
  - A leader encourages people to join together
- Failures of Social Control
  - Indecisive officials encourages social action

Types of Crowds

- Casual
  - Temporary, passive, limited social involvement
- Conventional
  - Structured group as in waiting in line
- Solidaristic
  - Developed sense of unity such as a revival
- Expressive
  - Gathering to change mood, emotions, as in a concert
- Acting
  - Angry, violent group, as in a mob in a riot

Blumer: Becoming a Mob

- Restlessness
  - Rumors begin
- Significant event
  - People become preoccupied with an incident
- Milling
  - Collective discussion of the incident
- Focus
  - A specific aspect is defined
- Agreement
  - People agree on action

Riots, Panics, Rumors

- Riot
  - A large scale violent collection action
    - Source is shared anger, frustration, and deprivation
- Panic
  - Collective but irrational reaction to a threat
    - Faced with a crisis, people become hysterical
- Rumor
  - A false report communicated from one to another
    - As it spreads, it becomes exaggerated and difficult to verify

Contagion Theory

- A crowd "catches" an emotion
  - A mutual stimulation of people seeing each other engaging in normative violations
  - "Collective mind" is less accepted today
    - Contagion still remains intriguing
    - Is mob construction a normal social reaction to an unusual set of circumstances?

Convergence Theory

- A crowd has prior unity
  - Crowd is formed by people who share certain similarities
    - Students' protest against an issue reflects the groups demographics or values
    - They already share similar opinions about the issue
  - Crowd may behave in unconventional ways
    - Actions would violate personal standards

Emergent Norm Theory

- Personal norms abandoned and replaced by group norms
  - In a crowd, people may become agitated and uncertain about what actions are appropriate
  - If group norm of nonviolence emerges, violators will be punished
    - If a norm of violence emerges, violent participants will be rewarded

Types of Social Movements

- Reform
  - Group attempts to change society in a limited way
    - Repeal a specific law
- Revolutionary
  - Group attempts to replace the existing order with a completely new order
    - Colonial revolution in 1776
- Resistance
  - Group attempts to stop or reverse changes that are taking place
    - Repeal of prohibition of alcohol in 1920s
- Expressive
  - Group attempts to provide gratification through self-expression
    - Religious movement: speak out and feel better

Relative Deprivation

- People perceive a gap between what should be and what is
  - One group compares itself with another and feels deprived
  - Social movement forms to make corrections
  - People more likely to participate as their conditions improve
    - Situation of rising expectations

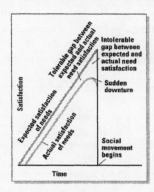

Resource Mobilization Theory

- Resources are the key to a successful social movement
  - Includes money, members, leaders, facilities
  - People must agree that the social movement is valid and legitimate
  - When times are prosperous, more resources are available
    - In deteriorating times, resources to support a movement become scarce

Mass Society Theory

- As a society industrializes it changes from a communal arrangement to an associational arrangement
  - Impersonal relations and social isolation
  - Absence of social ties produce alienation
- A social movement evolves to restore sense of community

The Civil Rights Movement

- End of Civil War did not end economic and political oppression of African Americans
  - Jim Crow laws
- NAACP founded in 1910
- Brown v. Board of Education 1954
- Dr. King and the SCLC
- Black Panthers and the Nation of Islam

The Women's Movement

- Feminists fight for right to vote 1840s
- WCTU and the crusade against alcohol
- Setbacks during the Great Depression
- Changes during World War II
- Equal Pay Act of 1963
- Civil Rights Act of 1964
- NOW 1970s

The Environmental Movement

- Three major factions
  - Mainstream ecology
    - Mainly work in formal organizations funded by independent financial contributions
  - Populist ecology
    - Emphasize individual and corporate responsibility
  - Radical ecology
    - Some follow Gaia
    - Some are ecofeminists

Changing Individuals

- Targeting individuals for change
  - Altering personal knowledge, values, and attitudes
  - Offering alternative through instruction
    - Formal instruction through schools, and other agents
    - Informal instruction through groups and group interaction

Changing Organizations

- Members participate in change
  - To what extent are members involved?
- Sensitivity to personal needs of members
  - Maintaining morale among members is critical
- Expectations
  - Positive encounters lead to cooperation
- Knowledge of operations
  - How will whole system be effected?

Changing Institutions
Gandhi's methods

- Negotiation without compromising fundamentals
- Prepare for action and consequences
- Demonstrate
- Repeat; refusal will lead to more actions
- Actions; strikes, boycotts
- Noncooperation
- Civil disobedience
- Take over government functions
- Establish parallel organization

CONCEPT WEB Collective
Social Action

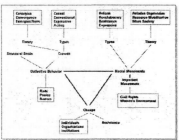